ANIMAL TRAVELLERS

Written by Jenny Wood

Illustrated by
Mike Atkinson, Jim Channell
and Robert Cook

HAMLYN

Published in 1993 by
Hamlyn Children's Books,
part of Reed Consumer Books,
Michelin House, 81 Fulham Road,
London SW3 6RB

Copyright © Reed Consumer Books Ltd 1993

All rights reserved. No part of the publication may be reproduced, stored in a retrieval system, or transmitted, in any form or by any means, electronic, mechanical, photocopying, recording or otherwise, without the prior permission of the copyright holders

Produced for Hamlyn Children's Books by Oyster Books

Consultant: Dr Julian Hector

Design: Designworks!, Cheltenham

ISBN 0 600 57360 5

Printed in Belgium

Contents

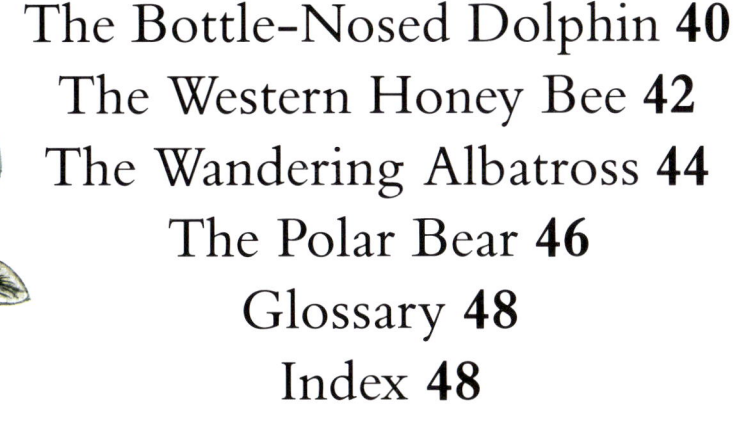

Introduction **5**
The Brindled Gnu **6**
The Desert Locust **8**
The Mouse-Eared Bat **10**
The American Spiny Lobster **12**
The Pacific Salmon **14**
The European Eel **16**
The Arctic Tern **18**
The Grey Whale **20**
The Green Turtle **22**
The Death's-Head Hawkmoth **24**
The Tropical Land Crab **26**
The Monarch Butterfly **28**
The Norway Lemming **30**
The Army Worm **32**
The Barn Swallow **34**
The Desert Ant **36**
The Ruby-Throated Hummingbird **38**
The Bottle-Nosed Dolphin **40**
The Western Honey Bee **42**
The Wandering Albatross **44**
The Polar Bear **46**
Glossary **48**
Index **48**

Introduction

For many animals, moving from place to place is an important part of their way of life. Some travel to avoid cold weather, while others go in search of new feeding or breeding grounds. Some travel to find mates. Others journey for thousands of kilometres simply to lay their eggs.

Many animals make journeys at regular times of the year. Some travel only short distances, but others travel half-way round the world and may cover millions of kilometres during their lifetimes. Although some of these long-distance travellers travel alone, many more join together to form large groups.

Regular journeys made by large numbers of animals are called migrations. Many migrations happen twice a year, as the animals move from their summer to their winter territories. Other migrations occur every day, between daytime and night-time territories. Some animals, such as the Pacific salmon, migrate only once and, once they have reached their destination, they die.

Long migrations can be very dangerous. As animals move out of familiar territory into unknown terrain, they often become easy prey to predators. Travelling in large groups offers protection, as the animals find safety in numbers.

The urge to migrate can be triggered by a change in the weather, a shortage of food or changes in the length of the day. Some animals may have an inbuilt time-clock which tells them when to begin their journeys.

Most animal travellers find their way using highly tuned navigational senses. Some are guided by the moon, the sun and the stars. Others follow natural features such as coastlines and rivers. Some animals are guided by the earth's magnetic field, while others follow scents borne on air or sea currents to help them reach their destination. Some animals, such as bats and dolphins, have highly developed sonar systems which they use to find a safe route. Many sea creatures swim with the ocean currents. Some animals use a mixture of these methods. Young animals learn migration routes by following the adults on their journeys.

There are many mysteries connected with animal travellers. How do some animals manage to navigate using the sun and moon, when these move across the sky? Why do some animals become lost on their migrations? There is still a great deal about animal migrations that scientists do not understand and may never know. What we do know is that travelling is vital to the survival of many animal species.

The Brindled Gnu

The giant herd is on the move. Dust churned up from the parched African grassland by thousands of hooves hangs thickly in the air. The leading animals reach the steep banks of a wide, sluggishly-flowing river. Pushed on by the press of creatures behind, they jump in. Soon the muddy waters are a chaos of struggling bodies. The banks on the far side become slippery as the leaders fight their way up the steep slope, dripping with water. Some animals, weakened by the effort of their great journey, lose their footing and slide back into the water. Too feeble to stand, they are trampled by the slashing hooves of other members of the jostling herd, and drown. Dozens of bodies float downstream, a grim reminder of the terrible cost of the great migration of the brindled gnus. Only the strongest survive the crossing and continue on their long journey.

The brindled gnu, also called the wildebeest, is a species of antelope which lives on the grasslands of Africa. When food and water become short, the gnus form herds and migrate in vast numbers to more fertile feeding grounds which may be thousands of kilometres away. They often travel six or seven abreast, in lines that may be 10 kilometres long. During the journey, males and females mate and, if the migration is late in the season, many calves may be born on the move. The young gnus have to learn to walk and keep up with the herd within a few hours. If they don't they will be killed by hyenas, lions and other predators which follow the herd in search of a meal.

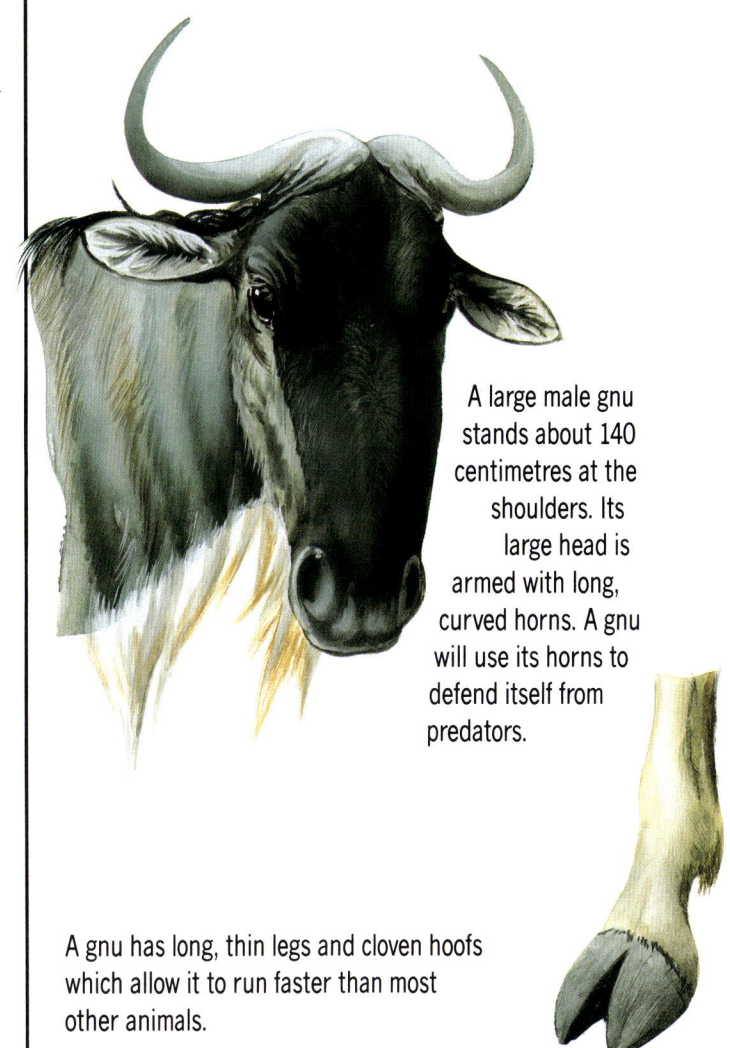

A large male gnu stands about 140 centimetres at the shoulders. Its large head is armed with long, curved horns. A gnu will use its horns to defend itself from predators.

A gnu has long, thin legs and cloven hoofs which allow it to run faster than most other animals.

Gnus range in colour from yellowish-brown to grey, and have dark vertical stripes on their shoulders and necks which act as a camouflage while the animals graze among the trees. Gnus eat mainly grass, but also leaves, fruit, flowers and seeds. They get their name from the grunting 'gnu, gnu' noise they make while on the move.

The Desert Locust

The rain has stopped, and the sky is once more clear and blue. The day promises to be fine and hot. But a dark cloud is forming on the horizon. It starts like a thin wisp of smoke but soon grows larger as it approaches, until its vastness blots out the sun. Soon the air above the fields is a blizzard of millions of flying creatures. Then the cloud begins to settle as the creatures swarm hungrily over the crops and the nearby trees and shrubs, transforming the landscape into a seething mass of feeding insects. Within a few hours everything green has been eaten by the marauders. Then, as if obeying a secret signal, the gigantic swarm of desert locusts takes to the air and flies away, leaving behind a scene of total devastation.

Locusts are a type of grasshopper. In hot, dry seasons the drab-coloured insects live solitary lives, feeding on the sparse desert vegetation. But under certain conditions, usually after heavy rain, a startling change takes place. The females, having feasted on the tender green grass which has sprouted on the once-parched earth, lay more eggs than usual. When the eggs hatch, the bright colours of the young hoppers which emerge are strikingly different from the drab colours of the previous generations. Not only that but, instead of being solitary creatures, these young grasshoppers begin to band together in large groups. When the larvae finally become flying adults, the groups join together into a gigantic swarm and fly off looking for food. A swarm may

travel for thousands of kilometres causing damage to food crops and other vegetation in its path. Eventually the swarm will die. Many generations of solitary locusts will be produced before the right conditions produce another swarm.

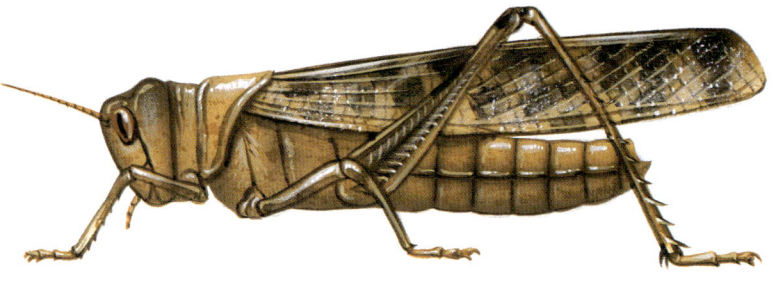

In its migrating form, the locust is about five centimetres long. It has two pairs of wings which fold over its back when it is not flying. It walks on six legs and uses its long hind legs for jumping. It uses its short front legs for holding food.

A female locust digs a hole in the ground with a special body part, called an ovipositor (egg placer), which is at the rear of her abdomen. Eggs pass out of her body through her ovipositor and into the hole. She makes a sticky material in her body which she sprays over the eggs to make a waterproof covering.

Locusts live in the hotter parts of Africa, the Middle East, the Americas and Australia. Most of the time they lead solitary lives but, when they swarm, they are considered a great pest by farmers because of the destruction they cause. All too often, locust swarms destroy vital food crops such as millet, on which hundreds, perhaps thousands of people depend.

A swarm may contain as many as 50,000 million locusts. A swarm of this size will cover an area of about 1,000 square kilometres and, in one day, will eat four times as much food as the population of London could consume in the same time.

The Mouse-Eared Bat

As the pale autumn sun sinks behind the trees, dark, shadowy shapes flit through the air, silhouetted against the darkening sky. They flicker through the branches and swoop towards the ground on leathery wings. These are mouse-eared bats, preparing to travel to their winter home far to the south. As they fly, the bats feed, snatching insects out of the air with their sharp, pointed teeth. Bats digest their food more quickly than most other mammals, so there is no danger of any members of this group carrying unnecessary extra weight on their long journey. The mouse-eared bats move ever southwards, travelling only a few kilometres each night. In a few weeks they will reach the warmer climate of their winter home.

Bats are found in every area of the world except at the Poles. There are over 900 species altogether. Bats are the only mammals which can sustain flapping flight although, compared to birds, they are not very efficient fliers. As a result, most species of bat do not migrate because they are not able to make long journeys on the wing. Instead they hibernate through the cold winter months, hanging upside down in caves or under the roofs of buildings. The mouse-eared bat, found mainly in Europe and North America, is one of the few species which does migrate. This migration takes many weeks. The bats fly a few kilometres each night, feeding as they go. They spend the days sleeping in places such as caves and hollow trees.

American mouse-eared bats fly about 3,000 kilometres each autumn to escape the winter cold. They fly only a few kilometres each night, averaging about 12 kilometres per hour, and rest every day. They spend the winter in warm places to the south.

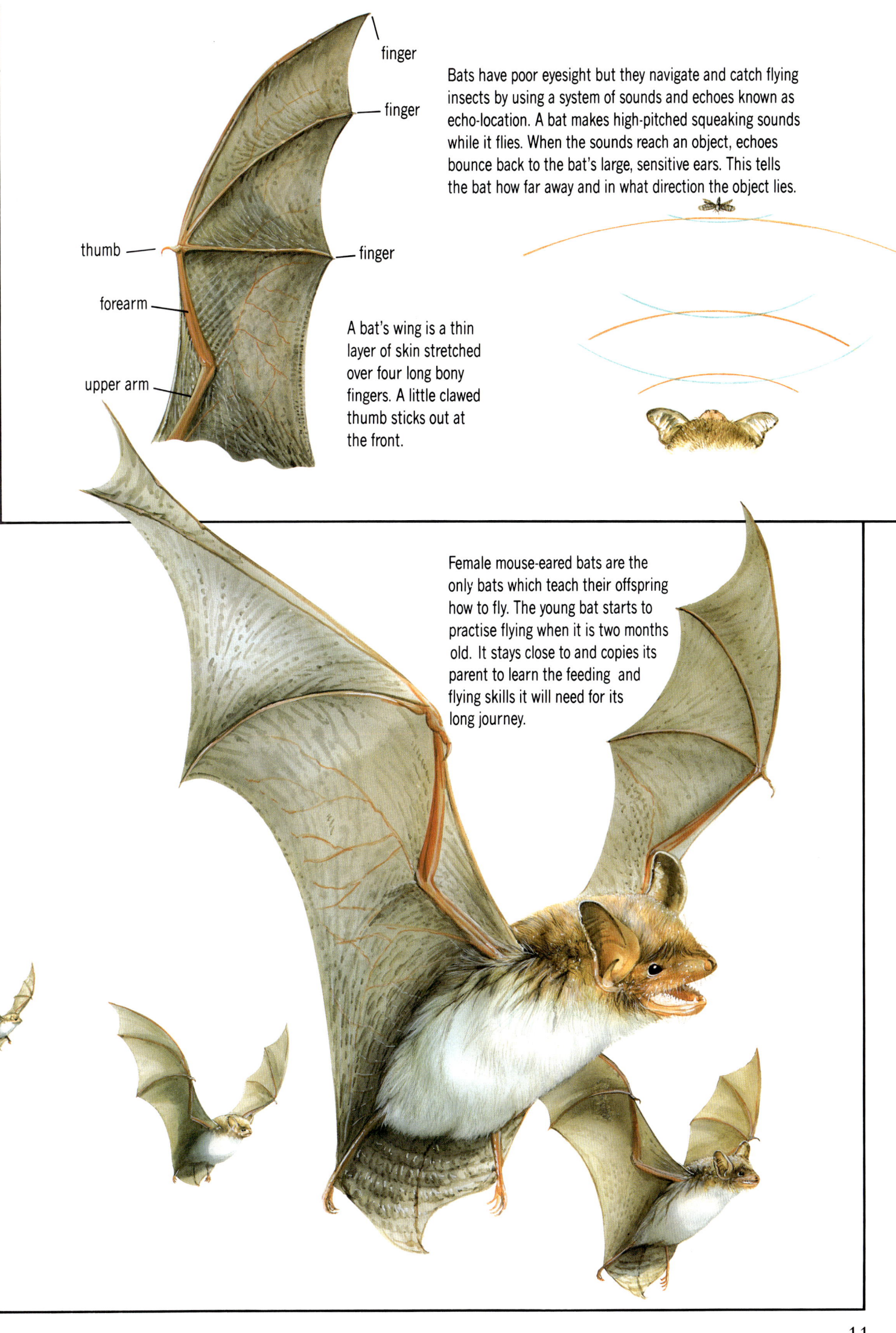

Bats have poor eyesight but they navigate and catch flying insects by using a system of sounds and echoes known as echo-location. A bat makes high-pitched squeaking sounds while it flies. When the sounds reach an object, echoes bounce back to the bat's large, sensitive ears. This tells the bat how far away and in what direction the object lies.

A bat's wing is a thin layer of skin stretched over four long bony fingers. A little clawed thumb sticks out at the front.

Female mouse-eared bats are the only bats which teach their offspring how to fly. The young bat starts to practise flying when it is two months old. It stays close to and copies its parent to learn the feeding and flying skills it will need for its long journey.

The American Spiny Lobster

Deep inside the dark hole on the sea bed a creature is stirring. Soon a dark, spiky shape glides out of the crevice and tiptoes across the rocks on its eight slender legs. Its spiky, armoured body

As it travels, each lobster keeps in line by using its sensitive antennae to touch the body of the lobster in front.

A lobster's shell is actually skin, toughened by calcium salts. This provides the lobster with good protection as well as acting as the creature's skeleton. As the lobster grows, it has to shed its skin. A chemical is produced inside the lobster's body which softens the shell. The shell expands and splits, exposing a new layer of skin underneath. This new skin is soft at first, so the lobster hides from its enemies until the skin hardens.

A lobster has two long antennae. Like the creature's legs and body, these antennae are covered with tiny hairs with which the lobster 'tastes' chemicals in the water to help it find food. The lobster also uses its antennae to feel things.

A lobster's eyes are located on the ends of long stalks. Each eye has hundreds of lenses.

scrapes softly over the stones. As it advances, the creature's constantly waving eye stalks keep watch for enemies. It moves towards a large group of identical animals milling about on the sea bed nearby. Gradually the creatures form a line, one behind the other. Then the line begins to move forward in a long procession. Soon the line is joined by other processions all moving over the sea bed in the same direction. The American spiny lobsters have begun their migration to warmer waters.

American spiny lobsters are hard-shelled creatures called crustaceans. They live in warm, shallow waters around the coasts of America. Unlike other lobsters, spiny lobsters have no pincers. They feed from dead creatures on the sea bed. The lobsters lead solitary lives for most of the year, hiding in cracks and holes in rocks. But in autumn, the lobsters join together for a spectacular mass migration south to warmer, deeper waters. They form chains of up to 50 individuals and walk across the sea bed to their new homes. As many as 100,000 lobsters may travel together, covering distances of up to 15 kilometres each day. The whole journey takes about a week. No one knows why these lobsters travel in long lines — perhaps it is just a case of follow-the-leader.

The Pacific Salmon

The rushing waters of the mighty river tear through the narrow canyon. As the racing tide crashes over the chaos of rocks, it produces a deafening roar. The large fish, already tired from its 3,000 kilometre journey, forces its streamlined body against the flow of water and swims into the powerful current. Its strong tail threshes and flails as it drives its painful way through the torrent. Leaping and twisting, the fish makes slow progress. Its red body is battered and bruised as the current sweeps it against the rocks. The fish is driven back time and time again before finally it wins through to the calmer waters beyond the rapids. The exhausted sockeye salmon swims wearily onwards on the last stage of its travel back to the pool where it was hatched four years before. Here it will spawn and then die.

The sockeye is one of several species of salmon which spend most of their adult lives in the Pacific Ocean. The life of a sockeye starts in the gravelly bed of a small stream many kilometres from the ocean, where it hatches from eggs laid by its mother. When the young fish are strong enough, they make the dangerous journey downstream to the ocean. Here they live for up to five years feeding on shrimps, squid and small fish. During their adult lives, sockeye salmon may swim far from the mouths of their home rivers. Yet when the time comes for them to spawn, the strongest of them fight their way back up-river to the very stream where they hatched.

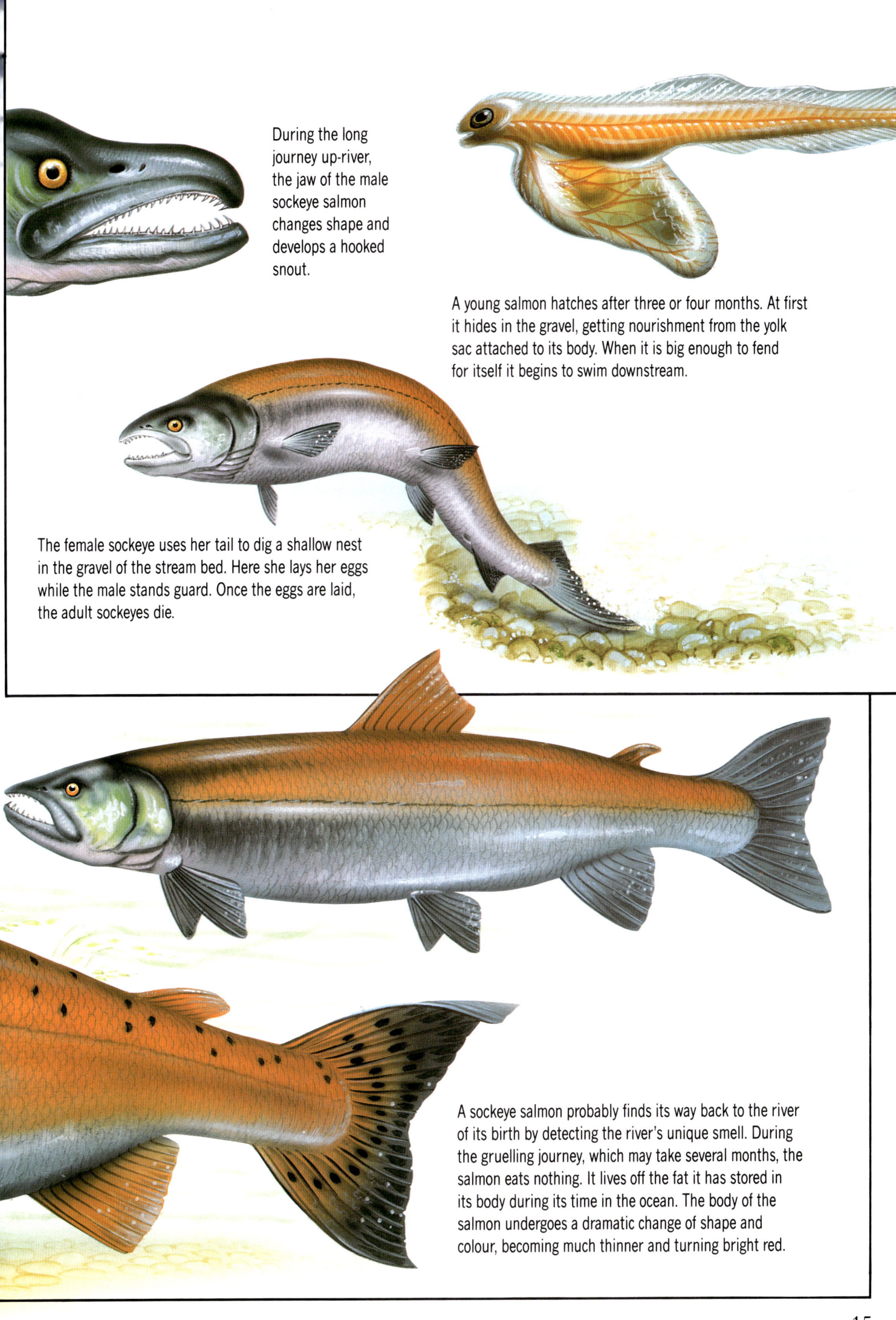

During the long journey up-river, the jaw of the male sockeye salmon changes shape and develops a hooked snout.

A young salmon hatches after three or four months. At first it hides in the gravel, getting nourishment from the yolk sac attached to its body. When it is big enough to fend for itself it begins to swim downstream.

The female sockeye uses her tail to dig a shallow nest in the gravel of the stream bed. Here she lays her eggs while the male stands guard. Once the eggs are laid, the adult sockeyes die.

A sockeye salmon probably finds its way back to the river of its birth by detecting the river's unique smell. During the gruelling journey, which may take several months, the salmon eats nothing. It lives off the fat it has stored in its body during its time in the ocean. The body of the salmon undergoes a dramatic change of shape and colour, becoming much thinner and turning bright red.

The European Eel

No one knows how European eels find their way to and from the Sargasso Sea. They may use their sense of smell or they may rely on ocean currents to give them their directions. Eels can detect the tiny electrical currents which are created by the movement of water. It is possible that they may use these electrical currents as signposts to help them find their way.

The cool night air is perfectly still. There is not a breath of wind, yet the blades of grass near the banks of the tiny stream are waving furiously. The disturbance is caused by several long, silvery shapes which wriggle and slide through the undergrowth then slip into the water. They power their way downstream, moving like finned snakes. They are joined along the way by others of their kind. When the seething, wriggling mass reaches the muddier water of a large river, the group swims strongly with the current and out into the open sea. The salt water makes no difference to their progress. Guided by their senses, the European eels turn south-west and begin their 8,000 kilometre swim to their breeding ground amongst the mass of seaweed floating in the distant Sargasso Sea.

The European eel, which looks and moves like a snake but is actually a fish, has one of the strangest life cycles in nature. These eels begin their lives as eggs in an area of the North Atlantic Ocean called the Sargasso Sea. The eggs, laid in spring, hatch into transparent, leaf-shaped larvae which are carried northwards by ocean currents. During their journey, the larvae change into tiny eels, called glass eels. At this stage the glass eels swim in different directions. Many of them head towards Europe. Gradually the glass eels grow larger, becoming silvery elvers. Male elvers probably stay in the sea, but the females swim into the fresh water of rivers and make their way far upstream. Once the elvers have become adult eels, they make the return journey back to the Sargasso Sea to breed and begin the cycle all over again.

It can take as long as 10 years for an elver to become a fully mature adult. Female adult European eels grow up to 120 centimetres long. Males are only half the size.

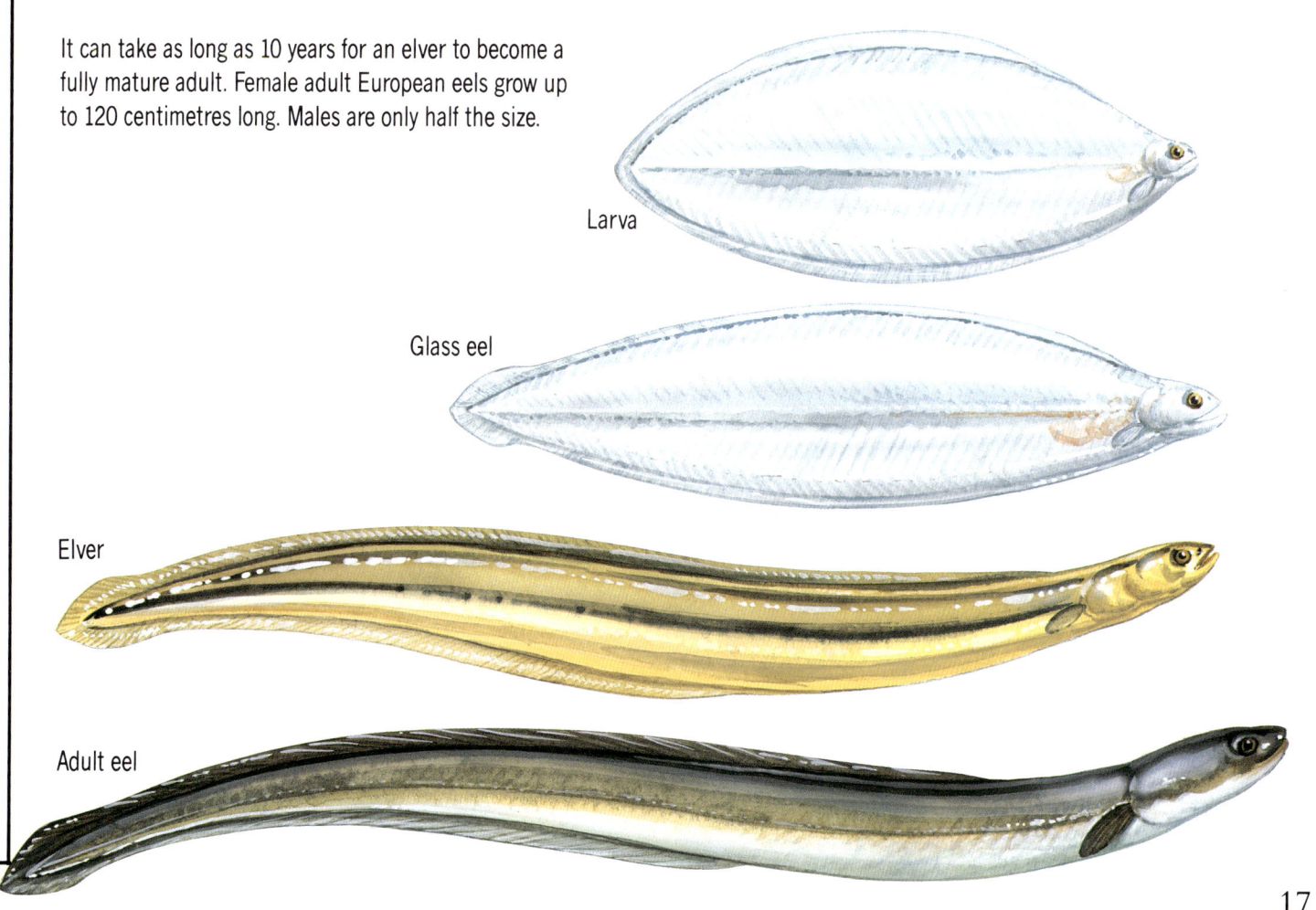

Larva

Glass eel

Elver

Adult eel

The Arctic Tern

During the summer at the Poles, the sun hardly dips below the horizon. By spending the summer in the Arctic and the summer in the Antarctic, the Arctic tern sees more daylight than any other living creature. The terns probably learned to make their incredible journey millions of years ago during the Ice Ages, when the polar ice caps were much closer together.

A cold wind blows from the north, whipping up white-topped waves on the surface of the green ocean. A grey and white bird dives towards the water, slashing the surface with her orange beak. She pulls out a struggling fish which she swallows whole. Spreading her delicate wings, the bird climbs higher then turns northwards once again. Ahead she sees the barren island, its mountains capped with snow. The bird flies along the sheer, rocky cliffs, until she spots a grassy plateau dotted with boulders. Banking towards it, she cruises along just above the ground searching for a suitable nesting site. The crowds of birds already there raise their heads and squawk aggressively as she flies over them. At last she finds an open space a short distance from the other birds, and lands. The epic journey of the Arctic tern is over.

The Arctic tern makes the longest migrations of all birds. During the summer months in the northern hemisphere, these terns nest inside the Arctic Circle in northern Europe, Asia and Alaska. They nest in huge, noisy colonies on pebble beaches and among rocks, defending their eggs fiercely. Once the chicks are old enough, the terns fly southwards for the Antarctic summer. When winter approaches, the terns fly north again, back to the Arctic. This journey, of about 16,000 kilometres each way, allows the terns to live through both the long Arctic and Antarctic summers and avoid the cold winter weather. During their journeys, the terns eat fish which they catch by diving at the water. By migrating, the terns take advantage of the best fishing seasons at both Poles, and always have plenty of food.

An Arctic tern has pointed wings which can carry it swiftly over long distances. A tern seldom soars but flies with steady wing beats, often with its head and bill pointed down instead of forwards.

Although terns have webbed feet and can float comfortably on the water, they are poor swimmers. A tern's feet are too small and weak to push it along quickly.

The Grey Whale

A gigantic creature glides through the cool Pacific waters, driven by powerful thrusts of its huge tail. It rises to the surface, breathing out in a fountain of spume. It cruises for a few minutes, the waves lapping its barnacle-encrusted body, then dives again in a welter of spray as its tail slaps on the surface. Within a minute the creature reaches the ocean floor. It swims along the sea bed, scooping up a huge mouthful of sand, then uses the horny plates in its mouth to strain out the crustaceans, small worms and plankton on which it lives. The grey whale accelerates through the water as the creature senses that its 20,000 kilometre journey will soon be over. Within a few days it will reach the food-rich, icy Arctic waters where it will spend the summer.

Grey whales live in the southern Pacific Ocean in winter then migrate northwards to the icy waters of the Bering Sea in spring. Here the waters are rich in plankton, the tiny sea creatures which form the major part of the grey whale's diet. During the summer months the whales eat large quantities of food and develop vast amounts of blubber which acts as an energy store for the long journey south. The whales arrive in the waters off southern California in December. Here they mate. In the spring they head north once more. Although the population of grey whales has been greatly reduced by whaling, there are thought to be about 20,000 of them taking part in this fantastic, long-distance journey.

Grey whales eat huge amounts of food every day so they usually travel alone, in pairs or in small groups. If a large number of grey whales migrated together, the sea through which they passed would not contain enough plankton to feed them all.

Grey whales are baleen whales. Instead of teeth a baleen whale has hundreds of thin, bony plates hanging from the roof of its mouth. These plates are called baleen and are made of the same material as human fingernails. Hairs on the inside of the plates act as a giant sieve to catch the plankton the whale gulps in.

The skin of an old grey whale is usually covered in barnacles, picked up during its long journeys. Tiny whale lice live among the barnacles.

The Green Turtle

Although a green turtle moves gracefully through the water, its great weight makes it very slow and clumsy on land.

A female green turtle may return to the beach at two-week intervals until she has laid up to three clutches of soft-shelled eggs in different nests. The eggs look just like ping-pong balls.

The sound of gentle waves slapping against the beach ripples through the still night air. All seems calm. Then suddenly an object becomes visible in the sea, moving towards the land. It is a green turtle. The turtle clambers out of the water on to the beach. She moves clumsily on this the final stage of her 2,000 kilometre journey, struggling to haul her heavy body over the sand. She advances laboriously up the beach until she reaches a point well above the high-tide mark. Then she starts to dig, scooping out a large hollow with her front flippers. She then lies in the hollow and uses her back flippers to form a smaller hole in which she lays her eggs. She stops only when there are nearly 100 of the white, spherical eggs lying in the bottom of the cavity. The turtle then scrapes sand over the eggs before lumbering back to the sea.

Turtles are reptiles which have shells. There are seven species of sea turtle which live in salt water. One of them is the green turtle, which lives most of its life in warm, shallow water, eating seaweed. Every year the female turtles travel enormous distances to various beaches in order to lay their eggs. Each female green turtle returns to exactly the same beach every year. Turtles which feed off the coast of Brazil, for example, travel to Ascension Island in the Indian Ocean to nest. No one is sure how the turtles find their way back to the same spot each year. They may navigate by the stars and the sun, or by sensing chemical smells in the water. These epic journeys can take several months because, although turtles are graceful swimmers capable of speeds up to 32 kilometres per hour, they tire quickly and move slowly most of the time.

When the baby turtles hatch, they have to dig their way out of the sand and then make their way to the sea. Although thousands of babies hatch, most of them are killed by predators. Many are eaten by lizards which discover the nest; or by crabs which intercept them as they cross the sand; or by sharks which eat them when they reach the water. The babies probably know where the water is because it is shiny. On beaches near towns, the babies often become confused by lights. They head in the wrong direction and quickly die of exhaustion.

The Death's-Head Hawkmoth

It is a warm summer night. Inside the bees' nest everything is quiet. The raider approaches the old oak tree on silent wings, hovering outside the entrance to the nest. Then it lands and pushes through the crack in the trunk, moving towards the centre of the hive. Before the sleepy bees can react, the large, dark shape is working on the honeycomb, sucking up the sweet honey with its long tongue. Slowly the nest comes to life as the bees realize that a thief is among them. The raider finishes feeding, moves to the entrance and takes off, pursued by a mob of angry bees. The thief accelerates away with powerful beats of its wings. The bees pursue but they have little chance of catching one of the fastest of all insects, the death's-head hawkmoth.

The death's-head hawkmoth lives in Europe, Asia and Africa. The caterpillars cannot develop unless the weather is very warm, so the adult moths move southwards to lay their eggs when winter approaches. In the spring, the newly hatched moths move northwards. These moths do not make their migration in one epic flight, but travel at a leisurely pace taking the whole season. On their journey the moths do not feed from nectar, like other moths, but on the sap of trees. They also raid bees' nests to steal the honey. The death's-head hawkmoth has very powerful wings and is thought to be one of the fastest flyers in the insect world. When threatened, it can put on great bursts of speed and has been timed at 54 kilometres per hour.

The death's-head hawkmoth gets its name from the markings on its thorax which resemble the shape of a human skull.

A death's-head hawkmoth sucks up sap or honey with its hollow tongue, or proboscis. The tongue is coiled under the moth's head when not in use.

The Tropical Land Crab

The night is hot and steamy. The tropical moon shining through the trees casts fantastic shadows on the ground. The crab races sideways over the forest floor, its eight legs working at incredible speed. Every few moments it pauses to look around. It pokes among the dead leaves with its big claw, transferring morsels of food to its mouth. Then it races on, its random progress bringing it ever closer to a group of terns sitting on their nests on the ground ahead. Seeing the approaching raider, the birds begin to squawk angrily. The crab rushes at an undefended nest, seizes an egg in its claw and races off. In the safety of long undergrowth, the tropical land crab cracks open the shell and eats the contents. Then off it runs, heading back towards its hiding place on the edge of the beach over a kilometre away.

Tropical land crabs spend most of their lives on land. They can do this because they have developed large, spongy gills which can breathe air.

There are over 4,500 species of crab, most of which live in the sea. Some species are able to leave the water for very long periods and hunt on land. These tropical land crabs are foragers which will eat almost anything they find. They scavenge across the forest floor, travelling as far as two kilometres from the sea. The crabs, which live mostly in the tropics in places such as the Bahamas, spend the day hiding under stones then emerge in the evening to hunt. During the mating season the crabs return to the sea in huge numbers to breed. In these mass migrations some species, such as ghost crabs, can actually drown if the weight of moving bodies holds them under the water too long.

Tropical land crabs come in many sizes and colours.

Blue land crabs will climb trees in search of prey.

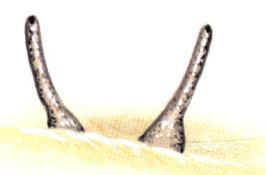

Ghost crabs burrow in the sand to hide from their enemies. They keep watch with their large eyes.

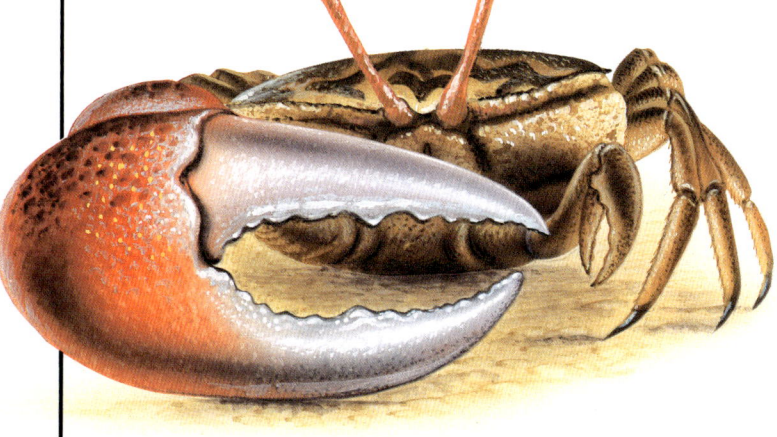

The male fiddler crab gets its name because one of its pincers is much larger than the other and looks something like a violin. Some crabs are left-pincered, and some are right-pincered! The crab waves its large claw to attract mates and warn away rivals.

27

The Monarch Butterfly

The cool breeze on the late summer day heralds the arrival of autumn. A group of fragile, long-distance travellers assembles on the trees around the clearing. Soon the air is thick with fluttering insect wings, creating a cloud of shimmering colour which wheels and spins in the air. The swarm grows larger, then takes off to begin the long journey south to Mexico. As it dances through the air, the group is joined by other swarms of insects until the whole sky is turned a brilliant orange by the flashing colours of their wings. The silent aerial procession of monarch butterflies, navigating by means of some unknown sense, moves steadily towards their hidden valley where they will spend the winter.

Monarch butterflies live in North America. They are the greatest of all insect travellers, making an amazing 3,200 kilometre journey south every winter. At the end of the trip they winter in a remote valley in Mexico, resting and feeding to gather their strength for the return flight. In the spring they set out again, but few of them ever reach their destination in North America. Most die on the way, but during the flight the females lay their eggs on milkweed plants. These plants are the only ones on which their caterpillars can feed. When the caterpillars turn into butterflies they continue the journey north. The descendants of these butterflies will make the next great journey south.

The life cycle of the monarch butterfly.

1 Egg

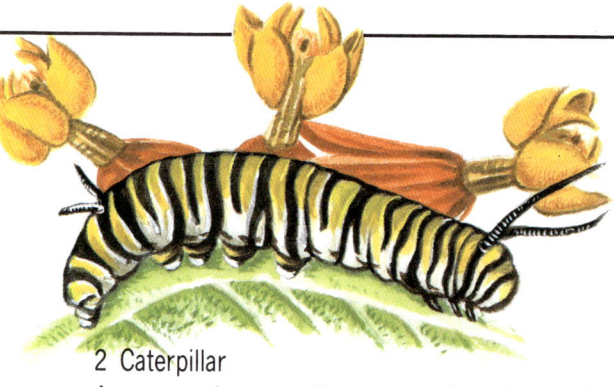

2 Caterpillar
As soon as the caterpillar emerges from the egg, it begins to eat. Monarch caterpillars feed on poisonous milkweed plants. The poison is stored in the caterpillar's body and remains in the adult butterfly.

3 Pupa
After about two weeks, the caterpillar becomes a pupa. During this stage the adult butterfly develops.

4 Adult monarch butterfly
The monarch is a member of a group of butterflies called milkweed butterflies. These are large, slow-flying butterflies with very short front legs. Adult monarchs are ready to fly within hours of emerging from the pupa.

Some monarch butterflies fly to Florida or California, but 14 million of them winter in one small valley in Mexico. The valley, which was only discovered in 1976, is in Michoacan State at an altitude of 3,000 metres.

The bright orange of an adult's wings warns birds and other predators that the butterfly is poisonous to eat. The monarch is the most poisonous of all the butterflies.

The Norway Lemming

The watery sun of late summer casts long, pale shadows across the Norwegian moorland. The ground everywhere is pitted with burrows. Hundreds of small, mouse-like creatures are crowded on the grass, feeding from the plants growing there. Suddenly, as if in response to a mysterious signal, one of the animals begins to run away from the group. More begin to follow, joining the rush from the overcrowded feeding grounds. Hundreds more join in the mad race until thousands of fleeing animals are boiling over the land like a flood. The procession reaches a river bank. The leaders can see green grass on the other side and plunge into the water. The lemmings swim desperately to reach the other side where they can find food. But the river is too wide and the water too cold, and they all drown.

Lemmings are rodents which live in forest and moorland areas in the cold, northern parts of the world, such as Scandinavia. They live in small family groups, marking their territory using scent glands and defending their homes from intruders by attacking any other lemmings who try to move into the area. But, since every female can have over twenty babies each year, lemmings breed at an astonishing rate. Every few years, their feeding grounds become overcrowded and there is a serious food shortage. This seems to cause panic among many of the lemmings who begin to move away from home in huge numbers, looking for a new food supply. Nothing halts the headlong flight. Almost all the fleeing lemmings die, either killed by predators or perishing in accidents such as falling over cliffs or drowning.

Lemmings live in underground burrows and feed mainly from fruits, seeds and plants which they find nearby. They line their nests with grass and moss.

The flight of the Norway lemmings seems like a kind of mad suicide wish. In fact it is a clever survival mechanism. Lemmings need to breed quickly in order to survive the harsh living conditions of their homeland. In certain years the population grows too quickly but the flight of many lemmings means that there is enough food for those which remain behind, and so the species survives.

The Army Worm

The heavy rainstorm is over and the ground is already beginning to dry in the hot sun. Green shoots are appearing everywhere, and the once-parched vegetation now looks green and fresh. A caterpillar begins to climb up a tree trunk. Soon it is joined by others exactly like it. Within a few minutes there are hundreds of caterpillars on the trunk. Within a few hours there are thousands. They swarm over the tree, eating the leaves and stripping the branches bare. Then, driven by their insatiable hunger, the caterpillars march down the trunk and join a mass of other caterpillars moving across the ground. Whatever plant lies in the path of this caterpillar army is soon covered and eaten until it is just bare twigs. The army moves silently, destroying all growing things in its path. Millions of legs carry hundreds of thousands of mouths to the next feeding site. The army worms are on the march.

Army worms are not worms at all. They are actually the caterpillars of the army worm moth which lives in Kenya and Malawi. The female moths lay their eggs under the soil. The eggs all hatch just before the rainy season begins. When the rains have ended, plants grow at a great rate. Then the caterpillars swarm to become an army of millions. As the army moves, it eats. The caterpillars destroy hundreds of hectares of vegetation. Army worms are feared by farmers even more than a plague of locusts because they do just as much damage but move completely silently. They can move into an area at night and be gone before morning, leaving behind nothing but destruction.

The army worm, like all caterpillars, has a tremendous appetite. When army worms swarm in their millions they can destroy vast areas of vegetation. They are a major pest in Central Africa.

The caterpillars eat until they pupate. Eventually they emerge as moths.

Army worm eggs always hatch at roughly the same time as the rains so the young caterpillars have plenty to eat.

The Barn Swallow

The autumn evening is cold and crisp. Mist forms over the fields. As the pale sun fades over the horizon, the birds begin to gather. They perch on telephone wires and on the roofs of nearby houses. Soon a great flock of twittering birds has assembled. As night falls, they spread their powerful wings and take off. They circle and wheel in the air, before setting off on their journey. Soon they are over the sea, flying southwards towards the warmer weather. Dawn finds them over France. As if obeying a silent signal, the flock descends, heading towards a large wood. The birds fly into the trees, searching for safe perches high in the branches. Here the barn swallows will sleep, safe from predators, until, having regained their strength, they resume their migration the following evening.

Barn swallows are small, insect-eating birds which live in most parts of the world, including the USA and Europe. During the summer months they move northwards to find nesting sites. In these cooler areas they can find plenty of insects to eat while they rear their young. In the winter the insects are scarcer, so the swallows fly south to warmer areas where food is plentiful. Some European barn swallows have been known to fly from Britain, across the Sahara Desert, to South Africa — a distance of over 9,000 kilometres. Barn swallows spend most of their lives flying and are perfectly adapted to catching insects on the wing. They are powerful, graceful fliers, with long, strong wings. When flying, barn swallows are very agile and can change direction in mid-air very easily.

Although a barn swallow has a small bill, it can open its mouth very wide. Small hairs inside the bill act as a fly scoop, trapping insects while the bird is on the wing.

The small, weak feet of the barn swallow are only suitable for perching, and are not very useful or efficient when the bird moves around on the ground.

Barn swallows are one of the few species of bird which have benefited from human activity. They use telephone wires and wire fences as perches and often build their nests under the eaves of buildings or in barns.

Barn swallows return to the same nesting site each year, sometimes repairing their old nests, but more often building new nests near the old ones.

The Desert Ant

The air above the desert sand shimmers in the blistering heat. A lone ant races over the dune, its legs disturbing tiny grains of sand which trickle down the slope. The ant moves across the empty, featureless landscape without hesitation, carrying a dead cricket in its strong jaws. It has already marched over two kilometres and knows by the angle of the sun that it must be nearing its nest. Ahead it sees a hole between two rocks, and runs in. Inside the nest it joins a stream of other ants moving towards the central storage areas, each carrying a piece of food. Once there, the desert ant passes its prey to another worker then turns around to set out on another journey across the lonely desert.

Desert ants live in very hot areas in Africa, America and Australia. They are great travellers, covering several kilometres a day in their endless search for food. These ants mainly eat spiders, crickets, grasshoppers and other ants. Amazingly the desert ant is able to find its way back to its underground nest in spite of the lack of landmarks. It does this by an inbuilt navigation system. The ant instinctively knows the changing angle of the sun as it moves across the sky. It uses this information to find its way accurately back to its nest. If one ant finds a good source of food, it can lay a scent trail back to the nest which other ants can follow to bring in the rest of the food.

An ant's strong, curved jaw helps it grip food. An ant is very strong for its size and can lift 50 times its own weight.

One species of desert ant, called honeypot ants, live mainly on honey. Foragers gather honeydew from aphids and sap from plants which they then feed to workers who never leave the nest. These workers store the honeydew and sap in their swollen abdomens, becoming living honey pots. The 'honey pots' hang from the roof of the nest, feeding the other workers with drops of the sweet liquid.

Desert ants send foragers out from their underground nests to find food. Although these scouts travel great distances they have the ability to find their way back to their nests very easily.

The Ruby-Throated Hummingbird

Although the ruby-throat is one of the daintiest birds living in the USA, it is also one of the fastest fliers. Wind tunnel tests have shown that the bird can reach speeds of 190 kilometres per hour. Other tests have shown that the bird could not possibly store enough energy in its body to fly across the Gulf of Mexico. The birds have never read the report and continue to make the trip every year!

A group of tiny green birds flicker through the trees. They dart towards a bush covered with large red flowers. Here they hover, making quick darting movements as they dash from bloom to bloom to feed from the nectar. One adult female breaks away from the group and flies off. In a blur of speed her tiny, feathered shape darts across the beach. Her wings, which beat so fast that they are invisible to the human eye, make an angry humming sound like the noise of a giant wasp. Without hesitation the bird streaks over the sand, the sun flashing off her brightly-coloured plumage, and flies straight out to sea. It seems impossible that this tiny bird has enough energy or strength for a long journey over the ocean. Yet this ruby-throated hummingbird is just one of the thousands which make an annual migration across the Gulf of Mexico — a staggering 800 kilometre journey.

There are more than 300 species of hummingbird. Hummingbirds take their name from the humming noise made by their rapidly beating wings. The smallest hummingbird is no longer than a bumblebee and the largest is only 21 centimetres long. The ruby-throated hummingbird lives in the woods and swamps of the south-eastern parts of the USA. A fully grown adult bird is only 10 centimetres long but, like all hummingbirds, the ruby-throat is a superb flier. Its wings, which beat at over 70 times a second, allow the bird to fly forward very fast, to hover and even to fly backwards. The adults build their nests in the spring and the female lays two eggs. These hatch within a fortnight and the baby birds can fly three weeks later. As soon as the young hatch, the males migrate for the winter. The females follow as soon as the young leave the nest. The young migrate alone.

A hummingbird will eat flying insects and small spiders, but feeds mainly on nectar from flowers. The bird hovers in front of the flower and thrusts its long, tubelike tongue deep into the flower to suck out the nectar.

The hummingbird's flying abilities are unique in the bird kingdom. Huge wing muscles, which take up about one-third of the bird's body weight, allow it to move its wings so fast that it can hover in the same place. The wings of some species can beat at over 200 beats per second.

The Bottle-Nosed Dolphin

An arrow-shaped formation of triangular fins scythes through the blue Pacific waters, moving at a tremendous rate. Long, streamlined, grey bodies leap effortlessly out of the water in curving arcs, creating a welter of foam. Then they plunge smoothly back into the water, their blunt beaks punching through the waves. The group is on the alert for food and scans the sea ahead for prey. The creatures communicate with each other as they travel by means of clicks and whistling noises. When a series of splashes and silver flashes betrays the presence of a shoal of fish, the travellers turn towards it. The group splits and begins herding the fish into a tight bunch by leaping and splashing round the edge of the shoal. Then the bottle-nosed dolphins race in to feed. Once the meal is over, the dolphins race off again, leaping and tumbling through the ocean.

Bottle-nosed dolphins are highly intelligent marine mammals which are perfectly developed for life in the sea. They live mainly in the North Atlantic Ocean and Mediterranean Sea. Each animal eats huge amounts of fish each day, so dolphins range for great distances in search of food. They travel in family groups called pods which can contain over 100 members. Members of the pod co-operate during the hunt, using their highly developed sonar systems to communicate with each other. Dolphins are powerful swimmers with long, torpedo-shaped bodies. Their streamlined shapes slip easily through the water driven along by their powerful tail fins. A dolphin breathes air through a nostril, or blowhole, in the top of its head so although it can dive deep, it will often swim along the surface.

Dolphins have between 100 and 200 sharp, pointed teeth which they use to grasp slippery prey. Dolphins do not chew their food, but swallow it whole. A dolphin will eat over 100 fish a day. Dolphins rely chiefly on their agility in the water to catch their prey.

Like whales, to whom they are related, dolphins must come to the surface of the ocean to breathe. A dolphin takes in air through a nostril, or blowhole, in the top of its head. Powerful muscles keep the blowhole closed while the dolphin is underwater.

Bottle-nosed dolphins can reach speeds of up to 25 kilometres per hour and can stay underwater for up to eight minutes. A fully grown adult can weigh as much as 400 kilos but is able to leap several metres out of the water. Wild dolphins are very playful and enjoy performing leaps and somersaults as they swim.

The Western Honey Bee

A bee performs a 'dance' as a way of telling other bees the whereabouts of a food source. The dance varies depending on how far away the food is. The figure-of-eight is used when the food is a long way away. A simple, circular dance is used when the food is very close. When the food is between 25 and 100 metres away, the bee does a combination of the two dances. The direction of the food source is indicated by the direction of the dance. The pitch of the buzzing may indicate the quality of the food.

The foraging bee buzzes through the warm, heavy, summer air. She flies on to a lavender bush and inspects the flowers which are heavy with nectar and pollen. The bee takes off again and flies back to the hive. Inside it is dark and stuffy. The bee makes her way to the wax honeycomb and begins to dance. She moves in a figure-of-eight, waggling her abdomen from side to side and buzzing loudly. The other bees gather round, 'listening' to the story she has to tell. They stroke her body with their antennae, picking up the scent of food trapped on the hairs there. When the dance ends, the bees leave the hive and fly without hesitation directly to the lavender bush. They begin to drink the nectar which they will make into honey and gather the pollen which they will take back to the hive. Soon the bush buzzes with the sound of dozens of honey bees, all brought to the spot by the travelling messenger.

There are more than 20,000 species of bee which live in almost all parts of the world except the very coldest places. Honey bees live in large colonies. A colony may contain as many as 80,000 bees and is made up of one queen, thousands of female workers and a few hundred male drones. The bees build nests, called hives. Inside their hive they build honeycombs out of wax which they produce from their bodies. In this honeycomb the queen lays her eggs and the bees store their honey. Honey bees often have to travel considerable distances from their hives to find nectar and pollen. The bees have developed a unique method to reduce the amount of time they have to spend travelling and searching for food. The bees send out scouts or foragers. When these foraging bees find a food source, they return to the hive and tell the other bees how to reach the food by doing a complicated dance.

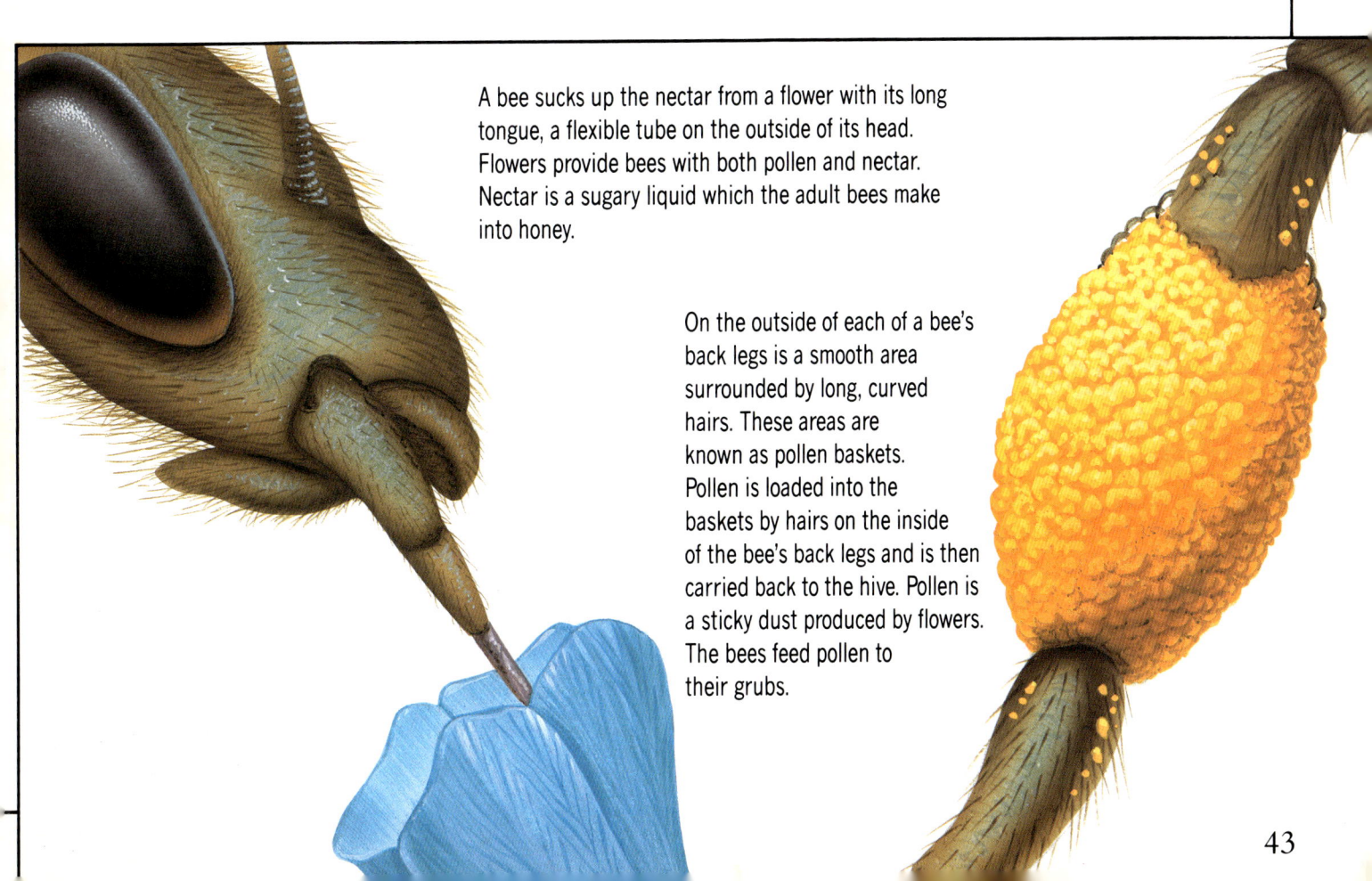

A bee sucks up the nectar from a flower with its long tongue, a flexible tube on the outside of its head. Flowers provide bees with both pollen and nectar. Nectar is a sugary liquid which the adult bees make into honey.

On the outside of each of a bee's back legs is a smooth area surrounded by long, curved hairs. These areas are known as pollen baskets. Pollen is loaded into the baskets by hairs on the inside of the bee's back legs and is then carried back to the hive. Pollen is a sticky dust produced by flowers. The bees feed pollen to their grubs.

The Wandering Albatross

The vast southern ocean stretches empty in every direction. A giant bird soars like a lone aircraft a few metres above the dark, rolling waves. The bird's long, narrow wings are outstretched and still, as it glides skilfully through the air. It wheels and circles, searching the surface of the sea for signs of food. Eventually the bird spots a promising movement in the water and spirals lazily downwards. The bird alights and sits comfortably on the waves, wings outstretched. Its long, heavy bill stabs into the water, pulling out a squid which it gulps down whole. Its hunger satisfied, the bird pauses briefly to preen its feathers before spreading its wings. With a great effort, the bird flaps slowly upwards then turns south towards a small, barren island. This is the breeding ground of the animal kingdom's greatest traveller — the wandering albatross.

Most albatrosses are found over the world's southern oceans. The wandering albatross is the largest of the species. Specimens have been caught which measure 3.6 metres from wingtip to wingtip. The wandering albatross can fly over 500 kilometres a day and over 200,000 kilometres in a year. During its lifetime it will circumnavigate the world many times. Albatrosses can sleep on the wing and only alight on the water to feed or to roost. They spend most of their lives flying and only land to mate. Although albatrosses have very few young, they make up for this by living a long time — possibly reaching 80 years of age. Albatrosses eat squid, but they are also scavengers which feed on floating carrion such as the bodies of seals and whales. A large carcass may attract several albatrosses which will cluster round and all feed at the same time, their wing tips touching.

Although an adult male wandering albatross can weigh up to 12 kilos, its enormous wingspan can easily carry it great distances.

Albatrosses have long, narrow, tapered wings which are perfectly designed for soaring. The birds ride the air currents with hardly a wing stroke. The wings are not very efficient for normal, flapping flight which explains why albatrosses are found over the windiest, roughest seas in the world.

Albatrosses breed on remote islands. The female lays a single egg in a hollow which has been dug on top of a mound of soil. The chick is born in summer and has to be fed throughout the winter. Chicks are not fully developed until the following summer. As a result, wandering albatrosses only breed every other year.

The Polar Bear

A polar bear's body is covered by a layer of fat and a thick, oily coat which can keep it warm in temperatures of minus 50 degrees C.

The Arctic summer is over, and the air is very cold. The huge, white, furry shape moves tirelessly over the smooth ice. Steamy puffs of breath come from the creature's black nose, the only dark spot on its otherwise perfectly camouflaged body. The animal moves steadily over a rougher section of the ice field, and soon arrives at a narrow stretch of sea. Without hesitation it plunges into the freezing water. It swims strongly, paddling with its front legs, and reaches the other side. Heaving its great bulk smoothly on to the ice, the giant bear pauses for a moment to shake the water from its coat in a huge shower of spray. Then the polar bear sets off again on its ceaseless patrol, smelling the air with its sensitive nostrils for the scent of a rival male.

Polar bears live on the ever-shifting ice fields of the Arctic. A bear cannot live in and guard one area of territory because the ice is always moving, so the males range for huge distances, travelling alone as far as 80 kilometres in a day. Polar bears may also venture a long way inland. They are perfectly adapted for their lives in the hostile ice desert near the North Pole. They are powerful creatures and ferocious hunters. They can run very fast across the ice and swim great distances in the freezing water. A polar bear's coat acts as an excellent camouflage against the ice. It has a tough outer layer of stiff hairs and a soft inner layer of shorter, woolly fur which insulates the bear against the cold. Polar bears have an excellent sense of smell and can detect food 15 kilometres away.

Polar bears have slightly webbed feet. Each foot has five long, curved claws which grip the slippery ice.

A pregnant female polar bear digs a den in the snow at the start of winter. Here she gives birth to a litter of cubs which she feeds on her milk until spring arrives. The tunnel leading into the den always slopes downwards, trapping the warm air inside.

Glossary and Index

abdomen The rear section of an insect's body. The abdomen contains the insect's stomach.

antennae Two long, thin 'feelers' found on the heads of some insects. Antennae are used for smelling and touching.

aphids Small insects which suck juices from plants.

blubber A thick layer of fat which forms beneath the skin of animals such as whales.

camouflage Any special shape or colouring which disguises a creature or helps it to hide from its enemies.

carrion The body and flesh of a dead animal or animals.

colony A group of animals which live together in an organized way. Each member of the group has a particular job to do, and there are rules to follow.

crustacea A group of animals which includes crabs, lobsters, shrimps and wood-lice. A crustacean has jointed limbs, and hard skin which acts as the creature's skeleton. Most crustacea live in water.

drone A male honey bee.

forage To search for, and carry away, food.

gills Special breathing organs found on some animals.

hibernate To sleep or remain inactive during the cold winter months, when food is scarce.

larvae The name given to young insects in their first stage of growth. The larval stage lasts from the time the insect leaves the egg until it becomes a pupa.

migration The movement of animals from one known destination to another, often at a specific time each year. These journeys are usually made in order to find food or to breed.

pincer A grasping claw.

predator A creature which lives by hunting other animals for food.

pupae The name given to young insects after they have passed through the larval stage. Pupae develop into adult insects.

sonar system A system of making, hearing and responding to sounds which is highly developed in animals such as dolphins and bats. These animals use sound to 'talk' to each other, to navigate and to find food.

spawn To lay eggs in water.

thorax The middle section of an insect's body.

---

abdomen 9, 37, 43, 48
albatross, wandering 44, 45
ant, desert 36, 37
ant, honeypot 37
antennae 12, 43, 48
aphids 37, 48
army worm 32, 33

baleen 21
bat, mouse-eared 10, 11
bear, Polar 46, 47
bee 25, 42, 43, 48
   western honey bee 42, 43
blubber 20, 48
butterfly, monarch 28, 29

camouflage 7, 47, 48
carrion 44, 48
caterpillar 25, 28, 32, 33
colony 19, 43, 48
crab, tropical land 26, 27
crustaceans 13, 20, 48

dolphin, bottle-nosed 40, 41
drone 43, 48

echo-location 11
eel, European 16, 17
eggs 5, 8, 9, 14, 15, 17, 19, 22, 23, 25, 26, 28, 32, 33, 39, 43, 45
electrical currents 16

feet, webbed 19, 47
forage 27, 37, 43, 48

gills 26, 48
gnu, brindled 6, 7

hawkmoth, death's head 24, 25
hibernate 10, 48
hummingbird, ruby-throated 38, 39

larvae 8, 17, 48
lemming, Norway 30, 31
lobster, American spiny 12, 13
locust 8, 9, 32
   desert locust 8, 9

migration 5, 6, 7, 10, 12, 13, 19, 20, 25, 27, 34, 39
moth, army worm 32

navigate 5, 11, 23, 28, 36, 48

ovipositor 9

pincers 13, 27
predators 5, 7, 23, 29, 30, 34
pupa 28, 33, 48

salmon, Pacific 5, 14, 15
sonar system 5, 40, 48
spawn 14, 48
swallow, barn 34, 35

tern 18, 19, 26
   Arctic tern 18, 19
turtle, green 22, 23
thorax 25, 48

whale 20, 21, 40, 44, 48
   grey whale 20, 21